From Your Grandfather

From Your Grandfather

A Gift of Memory for My Grandchild

LARK BOOKS

A Division of
Sterling Publishing Co., Inc.
New York

Created and produced by Lark Books
Text: Paige Gilchrist and Joe Rhatigan
Design: Kristi Pfeffer

AARP Books include a wide range of titles on health, personal finance, lifestyle, and other subjects to enrich the lives of 50+ Americans.

For more information, go to www.aarp.org/books

AARP, established in 1958, is a nonprofit, nonpartisan organization with more than 36 million members age 50 and older. The views expressed herein do not necessarily represent the policies of AARP and should not be construed as endorsements.

The AARP name and logo are registered trademarks of AARP, used under license to Sterling Publishing Co., Inc.

10 9 8 7 6 5 4 3 2 1

First Edition

Published by Sterling Publishing Co., Inc.
387 Park Avenue South, New York, N.Y. 10016

Distributed in Canada by Sterling Publishing,
c/o Canadian Manda Group, 165 Dufferin Street
Toronto, Ontario, Canada M6K 3H6

Distributed in the United Kingdom by GMC Distribution
Services, Castle Place, 166 High Street, Lewes, East Sussex,
England BN7 1XU

Distributed in Australia by Capricorn Link (Australia) Pty Ltd.,
P.O. Box 704, Windsor, NSW 2756 Australia

Manufactured in China

ISBN 13: 978-1-60059-093-1
ISBN 10: 1-60059-093-4

For information about custom editions, special sales, premium and
corporate purchases, please contact Sterling Special Sales
Department at 800-805-5489 or specialsales@sterlingpub.com.

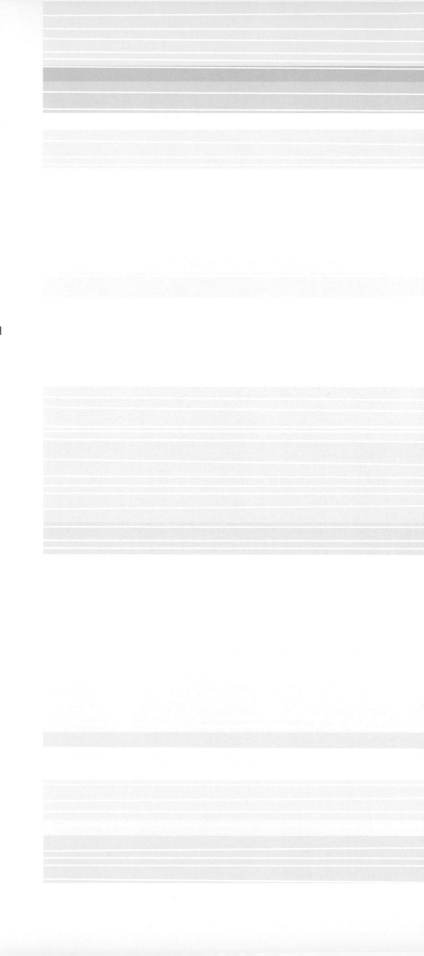

Contents

A Note to Grandfather

That's right. A note to *grandfather*. And that might feel like an odd word to use for yourself.

Grandfathers are venerable family patriarchs rocking on the front porch, not someone like you, who may be working at a full-time job, training for a half-marathon, serving on the city council, or building a shed in the backyard. But no matter how different your life is from your image of a grandfather—or from your own grandfathers' lives—some things will never change.

Throughout time, grandfathers have been the keepers of family history, heritage, and traditions—the family storytellers. When grandchildren come to visit, one of their favorite questions is still, "Grandpa, will you tell me a story?" It's only natural. And so is the fact that at some point, if it hasn't happened already, the question is going to change to, "Grandpa, will you tell me *your* story?" This book is for the telling.

From Your Grandfather lets you carry on a personal conversation with your grandchild, recording written and visual details as you go. You're guided easily through the process of reliving the past and reflecting on who you are today by helpful, fun-to-answer questions, voiced from the perspective of a curious grandchild. Straightforward fill-in-the-blanks invite specifics such as family-tree information and the details of your first job. And broader questions give you room to tell some of your favorite stories about everything from the fads, music, and cars that were popular when you were a teenager to the people who influenced you early on and the principles that guide you today.

The book gives you plenty of opportunity to personalize your approach to filling it out, making it truly your story. Many of the general questions come with prompts to help you get started. (*Tell me about college. What was your major? Were you in a fraternity? Did you work on the school newspaper?*) You can respond to them directly or toss out the prompts and even the question, and use the space to write about what you did instead, such as flee to the nearest big city right after high school, eager to live on your own, or spend a year hitchhiking across the country.

Use the book to tell your story visually, too. It's filled with space for pasting photos and jotting down captions or quotes. You can also tuck in newspaper clippings, concert tickets, copies of old letters, and any other mementos and memorabilia you want to pass on.

From Your Grandfather celebrates the story you and your grandchild share—a story that will help shape who he or she will grow up to be. It lets you relive some of your favorite times, offer your wisdom and experience, and watch your life come alive for that special person who wants to know all about it. Use this book to record the conversation—one that continues every time your grandchild asks the question that has echoed for generations, "Grandpa, will you tell me more?"

Put a photo of
yourself here

Tell Me About You

Your name (first, middle, last)

Were you named after anyone?

_____

_____

_____

Do you have any nicknames? How did you get them?

_____

_____

_____

I call you _____. Where does that name come from?

Who are you besides my grandfather?
Businessperson, traveler, photographer, hiker, volunteer, musician?

_____

_____

Your Current Favorites

_____
Books (or other things to read)

_____
Music

_____
Vacation spot

_____
Way to goof off

_____
Sports to play or watch

_____
Movies or TV shows

_____
Foods

_____
Thing to collect

_____
Political, religious, or social cause

_____
Part about being the age you are now

Why did you decide to create this book for me?

_____
_____
_____
_____
_____
_____
_____
_____
_____
_____
_____
_____
_____
_____
_____
_____

PHOTO PAGE
Put a photo of you
and your grandchild
on this page

me

_____
Name

_____
Birth date

_____
Place of birth

_____
Name

_____
Birth date

_____
Place of birth

_____
Name

_____
Birth date

_____
Place of birth

my parents

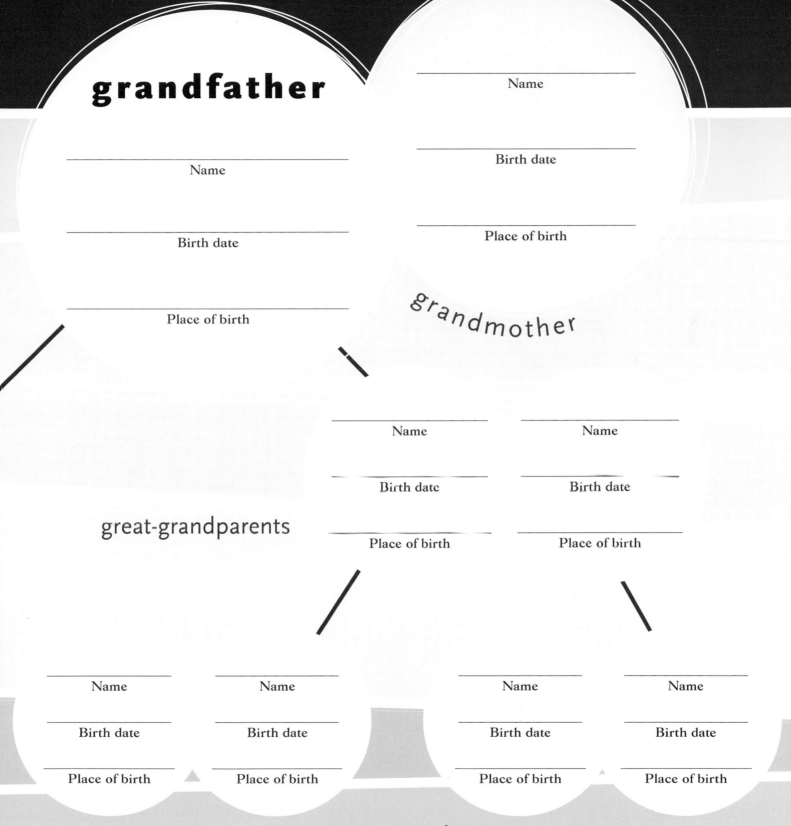

grandfather

Name

_____
Name

_____
Birth date

_____
Birth date

_____
Place of birth

_____
Place of birth

grandmother

great-grandparents

_____
Name

_____
Name

_____
Birth date

_____
Birth date

_____
Place of birth

_____
Place of birth

_____
Name

_____
Name

_____
Name

_____
Name

_____
Birth date

_____
Birth date

_____
Birth date

_____
Birth date

Place of birth

Place of birth

Place of birth

Place of birth

great-great-grandparents

What is my heritage?
Where are my ancestors from? When did they come to this country, and why?
Where did they settle and what did they do there?

Tell me about your mom and dad (my great-grandparents).
Where did they grow up? When did they get married? How did they earn their living?
What's something you'd like me to know about your mom? About your dad? What are
some of the most important things you learned from your parents?

PHOTO PAGE

Put a photo or photos
of your parents on this page,
and add captions if you like

Tell me about your grandparents (my great-great-grandparents).

When were they married? What did they do for a living, and how many kids did they have?
What do you remember most about them?

On your mother's side:

_____

_____

_____

_____

_____

_____

_____

_____

_____

_____

On your father's side:

_____

_____

_____

_____

_____

_____

_____

_____

_____

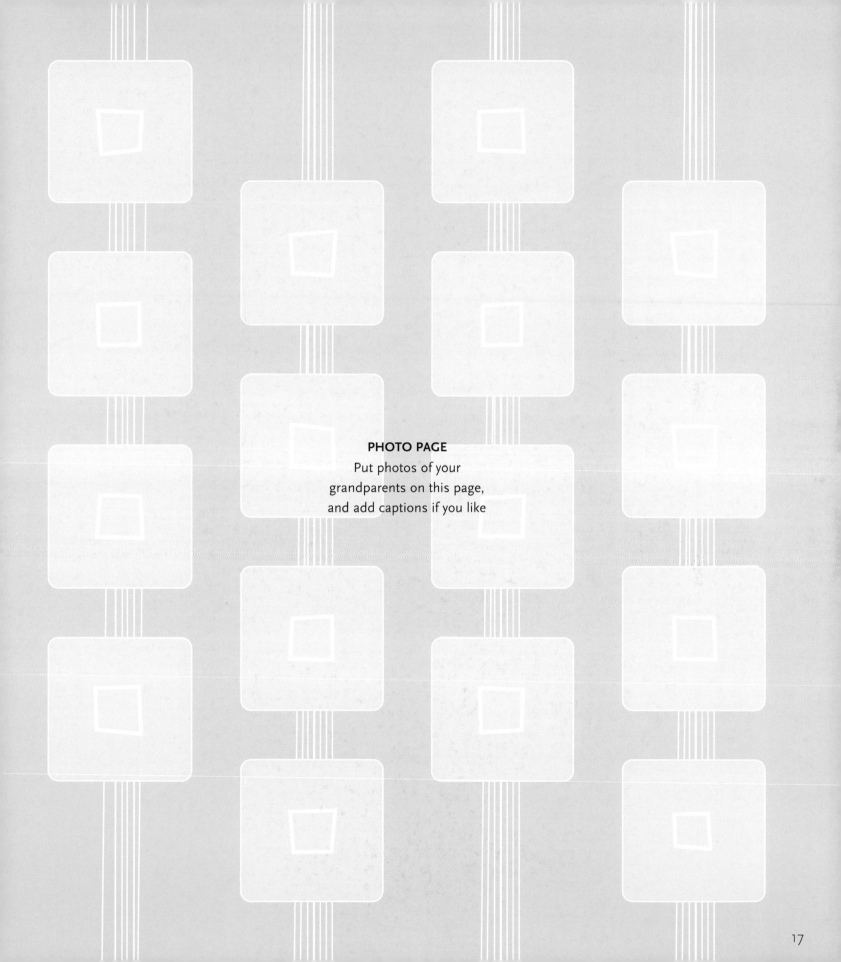

PHOTO PAGE
Put photos of your
grandparents on this page,
and add captions if you like

What about your brothers and sisters (my great-aunts and great-uncles)?

Did you all get along when you were growing up? What did you do together for fun? What's the most trouble you ever got into together (and what happened when your parents found out)? If you were an only child, what was that like? Were there cousins or friends who acted like siblings?

_____
Name

_____
Birth date

_____
Place of birth

_____
Name

_____
Birth date

_____
Place of birth

_____
Name

_____
Birth date

_____
Place of birth

_____
Name

_____
Birth date

_____
Place of birth

PHOTO PAGE
Put photos of your
siblings on this page,
and add captions
if you like

Tell me more about our family.
Who are some of our relatives everyone considers most successful? How about most interesting or eccentric?

_____

Who are the best family storytellers,
and what do they talk about?

_____

Who am I most like,
and why?

_____

Is there anyone famous
(or infamous) in our family?

When You Were a Little Boy

Where did you live?

Was it in a house, an apartment, on a farm? Did you move around a lot?

What was your family life like?

Were your parents strict? What were some household rules? What did your family do for vacations, trips, or other fun times together? Did you have family pets?

Tell me about elementary school.

What subjects and activities did you like most in school? Which were your least favorite?
Were you shy or outgoing? What sports did you play?

What about outside of school?

What games did you play with your friends? What were your favorite toys, books, or comics?
When did your family get a television? What were your favorite shows?

What were some of your favorite holidays, and how did your family celebrate them?
Any special decorating traditions? What about traditional meals or foods? Did you have a favorite
Halloween costume?

Who's the first president you remember?

Who were your heroes?

What did you think about being or doing when you grew up?

PHOTO PAGE

Put a photo or photos
of yourself when you were
little on this page, and
add captions if you like

What were you like in high school?

What were your favorite subjects? What activities did you participate in (sports teams, yearbook, band)? Who was your favorite teacher and what made him or her so special?

What was it cool to wear and do?

Clothes? Haircuts? Did you think you were cool back then?

PHOTO PAGE
Put a photo or photos
of yourself as a teenager
on this page, and add
captions if you like

Tell me about your social life.

What were some of the most fun (or wildest) things you and your friends did? Did you have a curfew? Did you break it?

What about dating?

Where did you go on dates? Do you remember your first date? Did you have a steady girlfriend or did you play the field?

_____
_____
_____
_____
_____
_____
_____
_____
_____
_____
_____
_____
_____
_____
_____
_____
_____
_____
_____
_____
_____
_____
_____
_____

What were the
popular hangouts?

What kind of music did you listen to?
Who were your favorite singers or bands? How about favorite songs? Did you buy a lot of records? Go to a lot of concerts? Play music with friends? What were the popular dances?

How about your first car?
What model was it? How much did it cost? Who taught you to drive, and how did that go?

Tell me about college.
Where did you go? What was your major? What activities (maybe a fraternity or the newspaper) were you involved in? What were you like—studious, a hippie, the life of the party, all three?

What was going on in the world?
Were you active in any social or political causes? Were there famous people—political leaders, activists, artists—who had a big influence on you?

_____

_____

_____

_____

_____

_____

_____

_____

_____

Did you pursue a career right after high school or college?
What were some of your earliest jobs? What was most challenging about the work you did then? Did you assume you'd have the same job or work for the same company your whole life?

PHOTO PAGE
Put a photo or photos
of yourself as a young
man on this page, and
add captions if you like

When You Married
My Grandmother

How did you meet my grandmother?
Where did you go on your first date? What did you like most about her then?

How did you propose? (Or maybe she proposed to you?)
Did you give her a ring? What did your parents say when you told them you were getting married?

All About Grandmother

_____

Name

_____

Parents

_____

_____

_____

Brothers and sisters

_____

_____

Where she grew up

_____

When she graduated from high school

_____

_____

_____

What she did afterward

Your Wedding

_____

Date

_____

Time

_____

Place

_____

Best man

_____

_____

_____

_____

Songs that were played

_____

_____

_____

_____

The reception

PHOTO PAGE
Put one of your
wedding photos here,
and add a caption
if you like

Who are some of the friends who helped you celebrate?

Best (or funniest or most nerve-racking) memory of the wedding day

The honeymoon

Becoming a
Dad

Tell me about when my parent was born.

When? Where? What do you remember about that day?

What was my parent like as a small child? As a teenager?

What are some of my parent's talents and gifts that you noticed early on? What are some things my parent did in childhood or as a teenager that made you happy? How about some that drove you crazy? What did you think my parent might grow up to be?

Put a photo of
yourself as a
young father here

What were some of the things you liked best about being a dad when my parent was a child? What were some of the toughest things?

PHOTO PAGE
Put a photo or photos of you and your child on this page, and add captions if you like

In what ways do I remind you of my parent?

In what ways am I different?

What are some of the things that make you proud of my parent today?

When I Was Born

How did my parents tell you I was on the way, and what was your reaction?

_____

_____

_____

_____

_____

_____

_____

_____

_____

_____

When did you first meet me?

Do you remember how you felt when you held me for the first time? When you bragged about me afterward, what did you say? Did you think I resembled anyone in the family?

_____

_____

_____

_____

_____

_____

Put a photo of
you and your
grandbaby here

What do you like best about being a grandfather?

What has surprised you?

How has being a grandfather changed you?

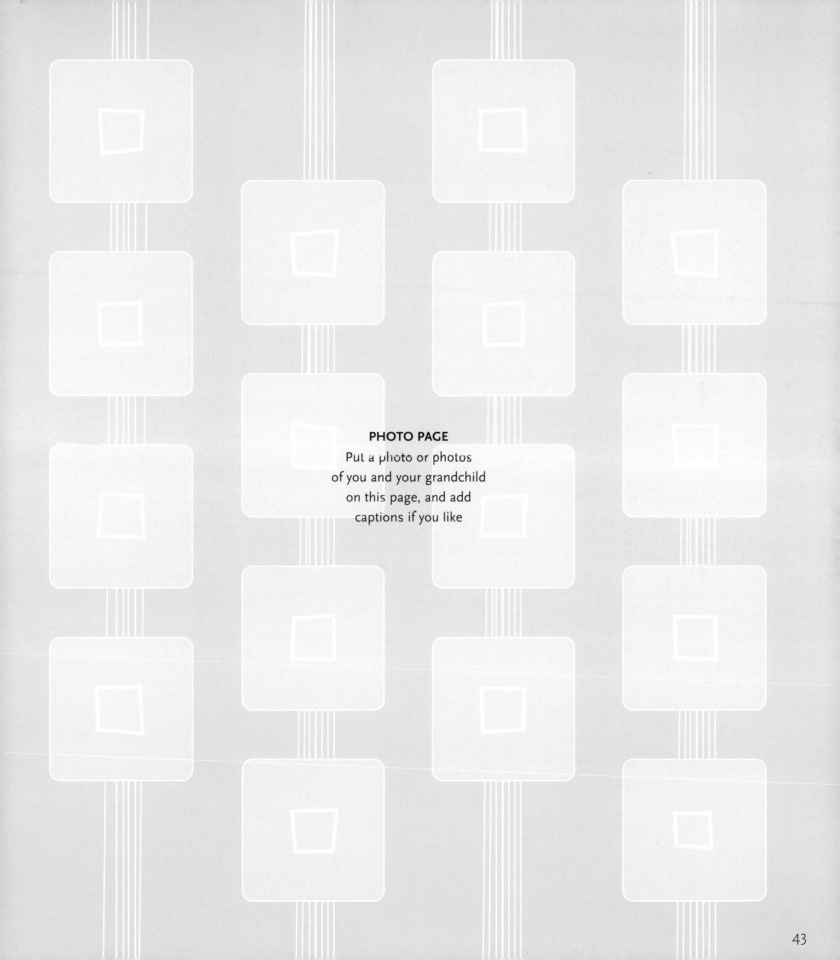

PHOTO PAGE

Put a photo or photos
of you and your grandchild
on this page, and add
captions if you like

Traditions

Of all the holidays our family celebrates, which are your favorites? Where do our traditions come from?

Are some of our traditions from when you were a little boy or when my parent was little?

What family dishes do we always serve?

What about any special rituals, such as decorating a tree together or churning ice cream on the porch?

First

Pet

Best friend

Trip somewhere on your own

Place you lived on your own

Presidential candidate you ever voted for

Photos • Mementos • Photos • Mementos

Photos • Mementos • Photos • Mementos

Favorite

Place you've ever lived

Car you've ever owned

Times spent with your children

Times spent with your grandchildren

Favorite

Places you've traveled to

Jobs you've had

Causes you've volunteered for

Quote

Photos • Mementos • Photos • Mementos

Most Important

Political or religious leaders in your lifetime

Social movements in your lifetime

Inventions or discoveries that have made your life better or easier

Role models or mentors in your life

Sources of strength or support in your life

Piece of advice you want to pass on to me

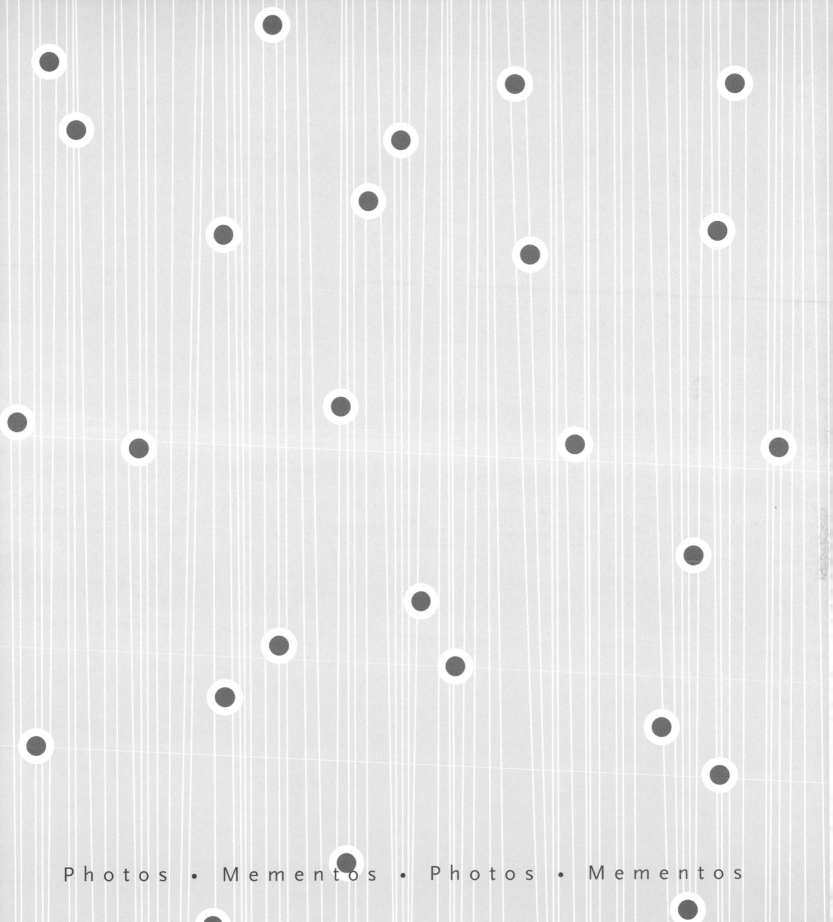

Photos • Mementos • Photos • Mementos

Photos • Mementos • Photos • Mementos

Biggest

Adventure you've had

Adventure you'd still like to have

Risks you've taken

World event in your lifetime—one so important that you remember
exactly where you were when you learned of it

Lessons you've learned

Accomplishment

Person Who

You looked up to most as a boy

You admire most now

You've learned the most from

Photos • Mementos • Photos • Mementos

Looking Back Now

Things you've found most important in life

The things people tend to make a big deal about that really aren't that important after all

Values you cherish

Principles that guide you

Experiences you hope I will have

_____

_____

_____

_____

_____

_____

_____

Traditions you would most like to pass on to me

_____

_____

_____

_____

_____

Never...

Always...

A Map of Your World

Tell me some of the memorable places you've lived, when you were there, and what you were doing, such as going to school, starting your first job, or settling into your first house and raising your family.

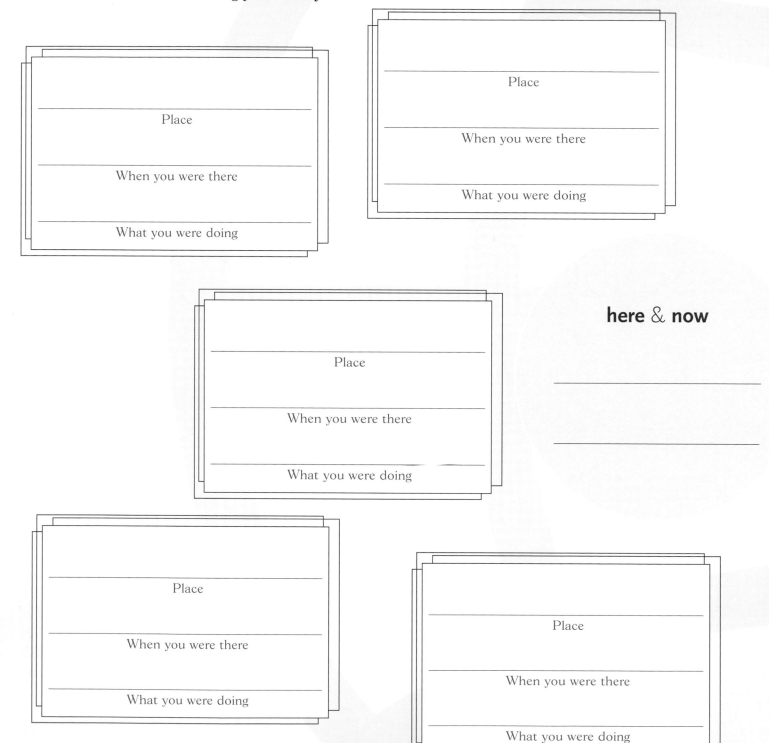

Place

When you were there

What you were doing

Place

When you were there

What you were doing

Place

When you were there

What you were doing

here & **now**

Place

When you were there

What you were doing

Place

When you were there

What you were doing

Place
_____
When you were there
_____
What you were doing

Place
_____
When you were there
_____
What you were doing

Place
_____
When you were there
_____
What you were doing

Place
_____
When you were there
_____
What you were doing

Place
_____
When you were there
_____
What you were doing

Place
_____
When you were there
_____
What you were doing

Place
_____
When you were there
_____
What you were doing

A Map of Your World

Fill these pages with photos of places you've lived, and add captions if you like.

Photos • Mementos • Photos • Mementos

Photos • Mementos • Photos • Mementos

Grandfather's
Words to Live By

When you're scared

When you're facing a tough decision

When life throws you a curve

When you're uncertain about the future

_____

_____

_____

_____

_____

_____

When you fall in love

When you have children or grandchildren of your own

When...

More Memories

Add more photos and life treasures on the next few pages.

Photos • Mementos • Photos • Mementos

Photos • Mementos • Photos • Mementos

Photos • Mementos • Photos • Mementos

Photos • Mementos • Photos • Mementos

Photos • Mementos • Photos • Mementos

Photos • Mementos • Photos • Mementos